The Green Goddess of Gardening
Patricia H. McLoud

Published 2019 by Shorehouse Books
Printed in the United States of America

ISBN-10: 0-9600085-4-3
ISBN-13: 978-0-9600085-4-4

Dedication

To my family and friends.

Acknowledgements

Thank you to Regina McLoud and C. Clayton Fox for their help with the typing of this book.

TABLE OF CONTENTS

Genesis

"The Lord God planted a garden in Eden and Eden was the place for the man he had formed" This is the record in Genesis.

This privilege of the earth has been man's since the beginning even though man has not realized it as such- and more often has ravaged rather than enjoyed.

In this hectic-paced life we lead, why is it that man does not stop and look at all that is his to enjoy? The plants were here countless generations before man, to feed upon, to enjoy, to use. Why does man not stop and look? Because he does not know how to choose and adapt these pleasures to his mode of life.

When planting a garden, a man may take a small space and adapt it to his own needs, or he may build against a native background. Whatever he chooses he will develop it as a testimony to his own emotions and skill.

Most people spend a great deal of leisure time in and around their homes. The joy experienced in planting a seed or plant and watching it grow to maturity, knowing that without your care and knowledge it would never thrive to maturity.

CHAPTER ONE

GOOD SOIL

OR

THE DIRT ON DIRT

THERE ARE THREE TYPES OF SOIL

SAND

Sandy soils warm up earlier in the spring and maintain a higher temperature than heavy soils. There are distinct advantages to sandy soil. Sand allows fertilizers to act more quickly in this type of soil. You can till their beds earlier in the spring months and they can be planted later into the fall months. Sandy soils quickly absorb irrigation which make it easier for you to dig or transplant but this type of soil does drain water quickly and might wash away nutrients at a rapid rate. You can improve sandy soil by adding topsoil, humus, peat moss, leaf compost or dehydrated cow manure all of which help to improve drainage.

CLAY

While frustrating for gardeners, clay soil, which is common throughout the United States, has some good qualities. It is more dense than other soil types so it retains moisture well and it is more nutrient rich than other soils.

The disadvantage of clay is the opposite side of the coin when it comes to retaining moisture: it doesn't drain easily. In fact, clay soils can be hard and concrete-like and difficult when a gardener wants to grow certain annuals, perennials or vegetables because many plants do not have strong enough roots to break through the clay composition.

However, clay soils can be improved before you plant. You can lighten the soil by adding topsoil and organic matter such as grass clippings, leaves, compost or dehydrated cow manure.

LOAM

Loam is soil composed mostly of sand, silt, and a smaller amount of clay. The soil's texture, especially its ability to retain nutrients and water are crucial. **Loam** soil is suitable for growing most plant varieties. Loamy soil is the best type of soil in that it is a mixture of sand and clay and organic matter.

ARE YOU WORRIED ABOUT YOUR SOIL DRAINAGE?

The correct drainage is vital to the growth and health of the plants. Here is an excellent test to determine adequate drainage:

Dig a hole into the soil and place an eight-inch clay pot (one with holes at the bottom) so that the top of the pot is level with the top of the soil. Fill the pot with water and see if the water will drain within 45 to 60 minutes. If it takes longer, the drainage must be improved. To improve drainage, add

Gypsum (Calcium Sulfate). This helps pull the soil particles together allowing better drainage. Spread two-to-four inches of the Gypsum over the soil and work it into the soil. Do this process two-to-three times per season checking the drainage between each application.

If the water in the clay pot drains too quickly, that is also a problem. To achieve adequate drainage, spread two-to-four inches of compost or dehydrated cow manure over the soil and work it into the soil. Do this two-to-three times per season always making sure to check the drainage between each application

SOIL CONSISTENCY

A good test to check the consistency of the soil is to take a clump of soil in your hand and then with your finger, tap the soil and see if it breaks apart without too much effort. This signals that the soil is of good consistency. If the soil breaks apart too quickly or without tapping or fails to break apart at all, your soil needs help.

So, what is the consistency of good soil?

One-part topsoil

One-part Soil Conditioner (Organic Matter)

One-part Lightener (sand, perlite or vermiculite

SOIL COLOR

Beware soil that is dark black. This may indicate that organic material has taken a turn into an anaerobic oxygen-less condition that is bad for the plant roots and beneficial organisms. Ideally, soil color should be a rich brown and not black.

Treat your soil with care. Try not to disturb or walk on it especially with flower gardens. It is highly recommended that you place flagstone paths throughout the garden area or stepping stones to minimize disturbing the soil.

BIOTA BACTERIA

Biota Bacteria is beneficial bacteria and fungi found in healthy productive soil. It helps grow bigger and better plants, and it repairs the soil by replacing the natural biota lost to chemicals, heat, cold, drought and frost. Nitrogen-fixing bacteria and biota make nutrients available to the rest of biota that would otherwise be locked up in the soil Without these crucial links, everything would die due to the lack of ability to uptake the precious nutrients.

SOIL pH

Soil pH measures the alkalinity or acidity levels of the soil. Soil pH measurements range from 0 to 14. Soils are known as Sweet or Alkaline if they measure above 7 on the pH scale. Soils are Sour or acidic if they measure below 7 on the pH scale. You need to find out where your soil lies before planting. Most plants like a slightly acid soil with a PH Of 5.5 to 6.5.

MAKING SOIL MORE ACIDIC

To make the soil more acidic add 1 to 2 inches of **Sphagnum Peat** to the soil in and around the plants. Sphagnum peat moss is partially decomposed remains of sphagnum moss which is found at the bottom of bogs.

MAKING THE SOIL MORE ALKALINE

pH should be raised for soils that lie on the low end of the pH scale (acid) so that plants have a better medium to grow

The pH may be raised by adding ground limestone. Go slow adding the limestone. Determine the rate of limestone addition by conducting acidity tests. Use Dolomite Limestone a little at a time. Take note that limestone can stay in the soil for about four years.

If a plant grows best in a slightly acidic soil, and the soil is already slightly acidic, no action is needed. But if the soil is alkaline, the plants will not be able to access the necessary nutrients in the soil.

To lower the pH of an alkaline soil, use finely powdered

Sulphur or aluminum sulfate. Make sure, as in raising the pH, that you test the soil.

Finally, adding an agent such as **Soil Moist** will help the soil remain wetter. Take care when adding a wetting agent to an already planted container.

When your testing is done and you have achieved the pH you desire, *m*easure your garden area, go to your favorite nursery, bring your soil information with you and ask which plants would be best suited for your garden. The nursery will also be able to tell you what soil treatment you will need to do for those plants.

SOIL MISHAPS HAPPEN TO US ALL!

A client called and said that her containers looked lovely, but she noticed a substance that looked like Jell-O® was all over her terrace. OOPS! Perhaps, I added too much soil moist? Could very well be.

CHAPTER TWO

HOW TO PLANT THAT PLANT

HOW DO YOU PLANT THAT SHRUB OR PERENNIAL RECENTLY PURCHASED?

(Hopefully to be planted in good soil)

First dig a $5.00 hole for a $.50 plant.

The hole should be deep enough that when the plant is placed (still in its container) it fits in the hole and level with the top of the soil. Mix in some fertilizer with the soil. Now, remove the plant from its container. Check the condition of the root mass. Is the soil surrounding the roots nice and loose? Or are the plant roots tightly surrounding the sides and bottom very thick and tight? If they are thick and tight, take a sharp knife and score the sides and loosen the roots at the base of the plant to allow the roots to spread into the surrounding soil. Sometimes it is advisable to remove about one half inch of this mass from the base of the plant with hands or a knife.

Now the plant is ready for the actual planting. Fill the planting hole with water. Place the plant in the hole and add soil. Pack the soil tightly all around the plant making sure there are no air pockets and add more water. When planting a balled and burlap-wrapped shrub or tree, remove the burlap first carefully in order to keep the root ball intact.

PERENNIAL GARDENS OF PERFECTION:

Perennial gardens are a source of pride and joy for gardeners. As with all gardens, you have to prepare the soil. The best time to do this is in the fall for spring planting.

SOIL PREPARATION FOR A PERENNIAL GARDEN

This is as good as time as any to discuss soil preparation for a perennial garden. The best time for soil preparation is in the Fall months for Spring planting.

First, if the area is grassy, remove all the sod. Hold onto these pieces and use to repair bare spots in your lawn.

Rototill to a depth of 15 to 18 inches. Remove any remaining weeds. Add the necessary fertilizers and organic matter to the area and rototill again. Collect one quarter to one half cup of soil from various parts from where you rototilled and place samples in a sealed bag. Label them as "perennial garden soil sample" and send them to a soil expert for pH testing or purchase a pH test kit which can be found at most garden centers. When you have your results, bring them to your garden center or nursery with your garden dimensions and they will tell you how much fertilizer and soil lightener to use.

Next, add a weed preventer such as Preen over the soil and leave undisturbed for two weeks. Products like Preen kill the weed seeds as they emerge from the soil. As you pull weeds from the soil, you might release weed seeds and the weed preventer prevents them from germinating.

When Preen is used, do not plant flower or vegetable seeds only plant rooted plants. In the early Spring, scatter a plant food like Plant-tone over the area and rototill. For an established perennial garden to give soil a boost, every two to three years in the Fall, scatter some top soil mixed with dehydrated cow manure over the garden.

The garden is now ready to be planted. Yes, it is a lot of preparation work, but it will be all worth it. After planting, perennials do not require or need a great deal of fertilizer. For an established perennial garden, spread Plant-tone in the Spring. In January or February, add an application of granular Super Phosphate (a bloom booster fertilizer) as this is important in developing beautiful flowers for the Spring, Summer and Fall.

Note: Granular Super Phosphate is not usually available in the winter so purchase it in the summer or fall so you have it on hand.

You need only a light application. Fill a metal coffee container with the fertilizer and throw the contents over the garden. If there is snow on the ground, ignore it and just sprinkle the fertilizer. Every two to three years in the fall months add a light top dressing of good top soil and Lime over the garden to keep it at its blooming best.

DESIGNING MY GARDEN

The watchwords for all beautiful gardens: Simplicity, repetition and harmony.

Perennial gardens require about six to seven hours of sunlight for flowering plants. There are many good choices for the placement of the garden. One is against an evergreen hedge that is slender in growth and will not over power the plants. Another option is against an outbuilding or garage or along a walkway or against a stone wall or perhaps an island garden bed. The size of the garden will depend upon the budget and the time required for the upkeep. Your garden is always a work in progress.

To help determine the size and configuration of a garden, use a garden hose to shape and add curves to your garden.

WHAT WILL I GROW?

Select plants that will bloom in the three seasons of spring, summer and fall. Plant in groups of threes and fives as this makes a visual impact.

Choose colors carefully. For example, an all-white garden can be dynamic but you might want it as a background color and blend other colors to maximize your garden's beauty. Careful placement should be given to groups of blues and purples as they tend to recede and get lost to the eye.

Think about the edging around your garden. It is just as important as the flowers. Two rows of brick or a similar edging not only adds aesthetically but protects your flowers from lawn mowers and other garden tools.

■■

There was a serious situation at the Philadelphia Flower Show. An exhibitor was delayed, and she did not arrive in time to place her exhibit. By rule, each class must have four exhibits in order to qualify for judging. Over the loudspeaker I heard "Pat McLoud report to the chairman of arrangements." I was asked to somehow get an arrangement together. I knew I had to improvise. I went to my car to see what I could find and to everyone's amazement, I returned carrying my new, shiny car jack. Someone handed me some lovely white Lilies and large green leaves which I used to get an original arrangement together. It passed for judging and completed the necessary four exhibits.

CHAPTER THREE

WATERING THOSE PLANTS

To water or not to water. That is the big question.

Watering, of course, is necessary for the health and growth of all plants. Plants like to be watered and then to dry out. They do not want to be continually saturated or continually too dry.

Weather of course plays a big role in the watering process. When it rains you may think: well, no watering today. That might be a mistake. But how do you know exactly how much rain penetrated the soil? There are rain gauges to help you answer that question. They are available at garden centers.

A glass jar or tin can will also suffice. Dig either one of these into the soil. Not too deep as you do not want to allow soil to get into it. This allows you to see how much it has rained.

In the chapter on soil, proper drainage was discussed which is vital to proper watering.

If you water too much or too little, you stress the plants and makes them weaker. Weak plants make them more susceptible to bugs, diseases plus they develop fewer blossoms.

There is a plant meter available at most garden centers. It can tell the wetness or dryness of the soil especially the indoor plants and also the outdoor containers.

WHEN TO WATER THE NEWLY PLANTED PERENNIAL GARDEN

Usually, you should water two times a week until the garden is established then cut it back to once a week. Always water thoroughly. Again, this depends upon the weather and amount of rainfall.

Water newly planted shrubs two times a week for about a month then water as necessary. Water thoroughly. Again, this depends upon the weather.

Make sure all plants go into the winter sufficiently watered.

In the Spring and Fall, when the evenings are cooler, water in the early morning or midday. This helps to discourage any fungus or mildew. In the Summer, you can water at any time of the day or night. In the past, it was believed that you should not water in mid- afternoon because there would be too much evaporation, but that's not believed to be the case anymore.

IRRIGATION SYSTEMS

After continually hauling many feet of heavy hoses, I decided that I needed an Irrigation system. If you want one of these, which system is best?

There are three types that I was familiar with. Soaker Hoses, Pop-Up Pipes and . Another that places the hoses vertically

.

Soaker hoses are difficult to place for all the plants to get equally watered. Also, the hoses are unsightly in the garden.

PVC Pop-Up Pipes are what their name says: they pop up and spray water over the gardens. After watering, they retreat to level ground. Therefore, there is nothing to break when working in the garden.

The vertical hoses are placed like an old-fashioned radiator and is the best system. But when planting new plants or transplanting old ones, it is easy to break a hose, and they are costly to repair.

I chose the Pop- up system.

***Do not leave pockets of depression around the perennials in the winter as water collects there and may rot the plants. Also, these pockets of water tend to freeze and defrost causing the plants to heave out of the soil

CHAPTER FOUR

FERTILIZING FLOWERS AND PLANTS

To Fertilize or Not to Fertilize: That is the Question

FERTILIZING FLOWERS and PLANTS

The numbers on the container are most important for the proper use of the fertilizer.

The first number states the amount of Nitrogen. Nitrogen develops above ground growth and gives the plant its dark green color. Also plant proteins and chlorophyll, essential for photosynthesis. The process of creating organic compounds(carbohydrates) required for growth. chlorophyll (green foliage) light, energy, carbon dioxide and water.

Too little nitrogen results in yellowing of the leaves, prominent vein structure and stunted growth. This indicates that the plant needs nitrogen. Too much nitrogen delays and sometimes inhibits flowering and fruiting often producing floppy plants. If this is a flowering plant, follow in three weeks with an application of soluble blossom booster.

The second number is Phosphate which develops flowering and good root growth. It also aids in maturity. Some granular super phosphate added to the planting hole of transplants is a good pick me up. A phosphate deficiency can inhibit flowering and fruiting or to drop prematurely.

The third number is potassium which develops strong stem and root growth This is especially important for tuber and root crops. Many vegetables and fruit trees require substantial amounts of Potassium.

Hydrogen and oxygen move these three nutrients through

the soil.

Super thrive is not a fertilizer but aids in the growth of plants. Follow the directions a little goes a long way I have had good results when using it.

Do not fertilize when the soil is very dry as it can create an overabundance of nutrients in the soil. This may lead to the burning of plant tissue.

Fertilizing the perennial garden

In the month of January or February even if there is snow on the ground. Scatter granular super phosphate over the entire garden also to the flowering shrubs. Do a light- to-medium application. This is important as it aids in the development of a beautiful blooming garden. Purchase the granular super phosphate in the summer as it is usually not available in the Fall or Winter.

Early in the Spring, scatter Plant-tone or another fertilizer over the garden and flowering shrubs. Water it in. Make sure you choose one that has equal amounts of nitrogen, phosphate and potassium. Such as 14_- 14 -14 OR 18-18-18 Around July   if you wish apply a light foliar feed with a soluble blossom booster to the garden. This may promote a second blooming. Especially to the early bloomers and those that have been cut back. Perennials do not require or like a lot of fertilizer. Do not fertilize in the fall.

Regarding Lilacs. In the spring, spread a moderate amount of lime around the base of the Lilac. Add a small amount of granular super phosphate before the lime. Do not add any other fertilizer at this time.

Annuals should be fertilized every two weeks with soluble blossom booster when used in the perennial garden If the annuals look dry water with clear water then with the fertilized water

Daffodils As soon as the shoots emerge from the soil use a low nitrogen fertilizer again in the Fall fertilize with Plant-tone.

Fertilize all other Spring bulbs after they bloom, again in the Fall also with Plant-tone.

Fertilizing Boxwoods and Hollies in the Fall is necessary to obtain a good green color. The fertilizer Urea is high in nitrogen which gives these plants good green color.

Fertilize deciduous trees and shrubs in the fall when the temperature is cool and there is usually regular rainfall. This allows the roots to grow and absorb the fertilizer. Which is sent to the leaves. When Spring arrives, the new leaves have a ready supply of nutrients. Use an all-purpose fertilizer. Such as Plant-tone.

Why fertilize Evergreens? If new growth is sparse or slow or needles do not have a healthy color. They probably need to be fertilized with Urea or an all-purpose fertilizer.

If the growth rate and needle color is normal. Usually fertilization is not necessary.

Regular fertilizing may be necessary if evergreens are grown in a less than healthy environment. Such as sandy or heavy clay soil or to encourage rapid growth to young evergreens.

Fertilize the grass in the Spring and more important in the Fall. Coast of Maine produces a product which is a mix of soil and fertilizer. Spread this on the grass Spring and Fall. Results are a healthy green lawn.

If there is a grub problem an application of grub killer is necessary. Use as directed.

Milorganite is also a good and inexpensive fertilizer. As I have stated before it is also a great deterrent to deer. if used to deter deer use it as necessary.

When the PH of the soil is below 6.0, phosphate gets locked in the soil particles. making it unavailable to the plants. An application of lime allows the phosphate to be available to the plants. Lime can last in the soil three to four years. Remember to test the soil.

There are kits at the garden centers to check the PH of soil. A soil sample can be sent to the state extension service.

Ironite is excellent for the vegetable garden. Work it into the soil Spring and Fall.

The fertilization directions for Container Gardening can be found in the chapter on container gardening

Always check the numbers on the container of fertilizer. Be sure it is the right fertilizer for the right results.

CHAPTER FIVE

MONTHLY FERTILIZING REMINDERS

January or February

Spread one half to three-quarters cup of granular Super Phosphate around the base of flowering shrubs. Also give a light dressing to species such as lilies purchased in late summer or early fall. Spread a light dressing all over perennial gardens. It is not necessary to water it in this time of year.

April

As soon as new growth starts in the spring, spread Plant-tone fertilizer over the entire perennial garden and around the base of flowering shrubs. Spread a cup of dehydrated cow manure and Plant-tone around the base of Hydrangeas.

Add a cup of ground limestone around the base of lilacs (only every three years or so).

Spread three-quarters cup of granular Super Phosphate around the base of Hydrangeas.

At the first sign of leaf growth on Roses, spread one-half to three-quarters cup of Rose fertilizer (such as Bayer Advanced Rose and Flower care) which feeds and protects against insects.

May

Fertilize Bearded Iris with a soluble Blossom Booster

keeping it away from the rhizome. To achieve, blue-flowering Hydrangeas, spread one cup of Aluminum Sulphate around the base of the plant in the first week of May. Repeat in two weeks and again in another two weeks. Water immediately. Spread one-half to three-quarters cup of Rose fertilizer around the base of Rose bushes. Always water the fertilizer into the soil except in winter months when the soil is frozen.

June

Fertilize Roses with Rose fertilizer and fertilize container plants weekly with soluble Blossom Booster.

July

Fertilize Roses with Rose fertilizer and Bearded Iris with soluble Blossom Booster Continue weekly fertilizing of container plants. Fertilize the Hydrangeas with soluble Blossom Booster

August

Fertilize the roses with rose fertilizer This is the last month to fertilize the roses with rose fertilizer. Continue fertilizing container plants weekly.

September

Continue to fertilize container plants

October

Spread one-half to three-quarters cup of granular Super Phosphate around the base of Roses

**Always water after adding granular Super Phosphate Or any fertilizer except in the winter months

***

A gentleman asked if I was available to design a garden for him. He asked if I could draw up plans for him. On my yellow legal pad, I drew arcs and lines and jotted down a smattering of notes. The gentleman looked at the drawing and remarked that he was confident everything would turn out well. A beautiful garden was born.

CHAPTER SIX

PESTS IN THE GARDEN

Gardeners worry about pests but the truth is that infertile soil or soil with little organic matter is responsible for most of plant problems. To avoid disease and encourage the vigor of plants, do not overwater or overfertilize and eliminate weeds.

BLACK SPOT AND FUNGUS

Neem Oil has proven to be a superior fungicide for the control of Black Spot and it also prevents rust from forming on Hollyhocks. It must be reapplied if it rains in the first 24 hours after application.

The most dangerous period for fungus to appear on plants is during May or early June when plants are growing rapidly and the foliage is soft.

APHIDS

Aphids can be a problem in the late spring. Aphids are small bugs that can cover buds and foliage. A strong spray from the hose can remove them. Adding Chive and Garlic plants help as they repel Aphids as well as destructive Beetles.

Another solution is the aspirin solution I mentioned in the chapter on tomatoes. Dissolve or crush one-and-a-half regular aspirin in a gallon of water. Spray it on the plants and then water the roots with the rest of the solution. Aspirin is a Salicylic Acid which triggers plants' natural defenses against bacteria and fungi. Use this solution once a month only as it can burn plants if overused.

SPIDER MITES

Spider Mites can destroy plants. They suck cell content from the leaves causing them to yellow, wither and fall from the plant. Spider Mites can come on quickly so look for the signs of a fine webbing covering the plants. If the leaves do not look healthy, check the undersides of the leaves. If it looks like salt has been sprinkled on the undersides, the plants have active spider mites. To get rid of them, use Oxamyl 10G which is a systemic granular pesticide. Repeat the application over and under the leaves every three weeks for four treatments. Make sure the label on the mixture you purchase specifically states it gets rid of Spider Mites.

MEALY BUGS

Mealy Bugs look like little wads of cotton on the plant, and they can drop from one plant to another. If you squish the bugs and they turn orange, the Mealy Bugs are alive. They usually do not kill the plant but they look awful.

Do not overwater or overfertilize plants as Mealy Bugs are attracted to plants with high nitrogen levels and soft growth.

Spray affected plants with Sevin as directed one time per week for four weeks. Do not use Sevin on food crops. Also, note that Sevin is detrimental to bees.

Another alternative is to spray with Safer's Insecticidal Soap four times every seven to ten days

Mealy Bugs can be the scourge of the greenhouse so spray all plants with Safer's once a month as a preventative.

Two weeks before taking plants into the house or greenhouse for the colder temperatures, it is a good practice to treat them to a thorough spraying of insecticidal soap

LILY LEAF BEETLE

The Lily Leaf Beetle attacks certain Lilies. This beetle has a black head and orange or red body. Evidence of the beetle includes holes in the leaves and this beetle will kill not only the present year's flowers but the next year's flowers as well. It the Lily Leaf Beetle is known to be prevalent in your region, spray the leaves with the insecticide Neem which is most effective in the prevention and control of the Lily Leaf Beetle. Apply it to the soil around the Lily. The Adult beetles can be knocked off the plant into a container of soapy water. When the new Lily leaves emerge in the spring, spray them with Bayer Advanced Rose and Flower Spray and also apply it to the soil around the Lily.

32

EARWIGS, SNAILS AND SLUGS

To deter earwigs, snails and slugs, spread Diatomaceous Earth in rings around the plants.

WHITE FLY

To combat White Fly, use a five-percent solution of baking soda with three tablespoons of Light Horticultural Oil in a gallon of water and add Knock Out, use as directed. This solution should get rid of White Flies. Neem is also effective against newly-hatched White Fly larvae.

Yellow sticky cards can also be used to trap the White Fly.

JAPANESE BEETLES

Garden naturals with Bonide can control Japanese Beetles and it can also be sprayed on vegetables and flowers.

THE ITCHY PESTS

To repel insects and keep them from biting you, put white vinegar on your arms or legs. Also, wear long-sleeved shirts and long pants. If you do get bit, rub meat tenderizer on the area. Do not use this remedy if the bite looks raw or shows signs of infection.

To repel mosquitoes, crush and rub Nepeta (cat mint) on your skin. Some experts say this is better than DEET.

And the most common-sense advice I can give: When approaching any garden or field area, check to see that there is no Poison Ivy. Poison Ivy has three shiny leaves. If you rub the crushed leaves, apply Zanfel.

ANOTHER SPRAY SOLUTION TO PREVENT AND KILL INSECTS

One more option in your quest to rid your garden of pests!

Two-and-a-half tablespoons of vegetable oil

Two-and-a-half tablespoons of dishwasher detergent (do not use one that has a grease cutter)

One Gallon of water

Mix and put in a sprayer. Always spray the top and undersides of leaves. If insects are present, spray once-a-day in the morning or evening for three weeks to effectively kill insects.

If there are no insects present, spray on the plants once a month as a preventative.

Weeds are pests as well, so a natural way to get rid of them is to mix one-gallon white vinegar with one pint of lemon juice (not concentrated). Spray on the weeds.

THE GARDENER'S REWARD

After a day in the garden, pour yourself a glass of wine or iced tea and wander the area admiring all your hard work. Please don't lean over to pull a weed. It won't hurt your flowers or vegetables but you will lose your drink!

***

THE GROUNDHOG

A ground hog came to live under our garden shed. What to do? We got a trap and some bait. We used cooked bacon as we heard it is good bait. So, to the kitchen I went. A few days went by with no results. Then one morning, we looked out an upstairs window and saw something in the trap. We rushed to the area of the trap. No ground hog, but we had trapped a large skunk. We got a long pole, opened the trap and off went the skunk We never saw that skunk or the ground hog again.

CHAPTER SEVEN
THE PROPER WAY TO PRUNE

Keeping plants and shrubs neat and trim is not just about looks but plant health too. Pruning is essential in order to keep the size and shape of the plant and to prevent unwanted growth. When I need my trees and large shrubs pruned, I call in the experts. Otherwise the pruning of small-to-medium-sized shrubs can be accomplished with the right tools.

If you have been fortunate to have purchased a house with a selection of interesting foundation plantings, in scale and proportion to the house you purchased, you should celebrate. You can enjoy your shrubbery, landscape and home's curb appeal.

If on the other hand, the foundation planting has grown out of control and overtaken the house, you have a challenge. What are your choices? You can remove it all and start over or try to prune and shape the shrubbery and plants without leaving large gaping holes in your landscape which can also ruin curb and backyard appeal. Remember, experts are out there to give direction on what plants will do well with pruning and what plants need to go.

If you prune yourself, prune flowering shrubs after they flower to ensure the next season's flowers. Keep the flowering shrubs to a controllable height and width so you can enjoy the flowers.

CHAPTER EIGHT

WHY MULCH?

Mulching not only helps retain water but it also helps deter weeds. Be sure to get a good grade of mulch that is free of weed seeds. I recommend shredded dark brown or black mulch, I do not recommend pine bark mulch because it comes in large pieces which makes it less attractive than the shredded variety.

MULCH TIPS

- Mulch should not be more than two-to-three-inches deep
- Keep mulch away from trunks of trees and the base of perennials, roses and all plants.
- Landscapers tend to spread mulch too deep and too often
- If there is a large, open area in front of the foundation, place plants rather than mulch in that area. Plants, especially groundcovers, are more attractive and provide wonderful curb appeal.
- River stone is sometimes used an alternative to mulch in certain areas of the garden.

CHAPTER NINE

PERENNNIAL GARDENS

OR

GARDENS OF PERFECTION

Perennial gardening is one of the most rewarding of gardens. All good gardens start with soil preparation. The best time to prepare the soil is in the Fall for Spring planting.

If the area selected is covered with grass, the first step is to remove that grass. Save the grass plugs for other barren areas in your yard.

Rototill the area to a depth of 15 to 18 inches. This is the ideal depth. Remove any remaining weeds that have surfaced. Test the PH of the soil by collecting one- quarter to one-half cups of soil from various sections that have been rototilled.

Place the soil in a sealed bag, label them "From a Proposed Perennial Garden" and send it off to the nearest extension service. Or you can use one of the available PH testers that can be purchased from a garden center. Bring the results to the garden center plus the dimensions of your perennial garden. The garden center will advise you on how much fertilizer, organic matter and lightener you might need for the proposed site. Be sure to bring the measurement of the proposed garden. Spread these soil conditioners over the proposed garden and rototill them in.

After this process, spread PREEM (a weed seed preventer) on top of the soil and gently water. Leave this area undisturbed for two weeks. PREEM kills any existing weed seeds. In early spring, spread Plant-tone fertilizer and rototill or use a spade. When PREEM is used, do not plant seeds— only rooted plants.

The garden is now ready to be planted. Yes, it has been a lot of labor to get to this point but it is well worth it when you see the results.

After planting, perennials, do not require or need a lot of fertilizer. To an established perennial garden, spread Plant-tone in the Spring. In January or February, put down an application of granular Super Phosphate (which is a bloom booster fertilizer). This is most important in developing beautiful, profuse flowers for the Spring, Summer and Fall. The Super Phosphate is not usually available in the Winter months so purchase it in the Summer or Fall.

A light application is all that is needed so purchase bags that make sense for the size of your garden.

To apply it, use a metal coffee can filled with fertilizer and throw the contents over the garden. If you are unsure of the amount to spread, consult with the experts at the garden center. If they say it is not needed, walk away. YOU NEED TO DO THIS! EVEN IF THERE IS SNOW ON THE GROUND—DO THE APPLICATION!!!

The perennial garden requires about six to seven hours of sunlight for flowering plants.

There are many good choices for the placement of the garden. For example, a garden against an evergreen hedge is a great option especially if that hedge is slender in growth and will not overpower the plants. Another great site is against an outbuilding or garage or along a walkway or against a stone wall or perhaps you might prefer an island bed.

The size of the garden will also depend upon your financial and time budgets. Perennial gardens are a work in process so select a size that will not overwhelm and the time available to maintain the garden.

Select plants that will bloom in Spring, Summer and Fall. Beware of invasive plants. Plant in groups of threes and fours as these groups make a definite impact to the eye.

Choose colors carefully. An all-white garden can be dynamic and a great background and a blender for other colors. Careful placement should be given to where groups of blues and purples are planted as they tend to recede and sometimes present as an empty space to the eye.

Two rows of brick are an attractive edging for your perennial garden and it also serves to keep the lawnmower away from the plants.

THE WATCHWORDS OF ALL BEAUTIFUL GARDENS:

SIMPLICITY REPETITION AND HARMONY

CHAPTER TEN

FLOWER FORMS IN THE GARDEN

OR

YOU ALL HAVE A GREAT SHAPE

When planting a garden, you want to create a symphony of both color and form so that the garden reflects its goals of simplicity, repetition and harmony. Plants offer so much diversity and here is a list to help you pick the right plants for the right locations in your garden.

Puffy Plant Forms:

These are flat ground-hugging plants. They are best used to fill the front of the garden and set off the upright plants they surround:

- Perennial Geranium "Rozanne"
- Low Sedums
- Dusty Miller
- Miniature Hosta
- Arabis
- Phlox "Subulata"
- Campanula (Low)
- Saponaria

Round Plant Forms:

These plants are often the most common forms in a garden. They can unify the garden by providing repetition and keeping eyes focused on all flowers.

- Shasta Daisy
- Echinacea

- Alliums Gigantum
- Iris Bearded
- Yarrow
- Iris Enstata
- Rudebecia "Cherokee"
- Phlox "David"
- Sedum Spectabile
- Peony

Billowing Plant Forms:

These plants can be used to link more dramatic plants together. They create a path for the eye to follow:

- Gypsophila "Baby's Breath"
- Boltonia
- Gaura
- Aruncus Goat's Beard
- Astible "Chinesis"
- Fillipendula Rubra
- Nepeta Six Hills Giant
- Thalictrum

DO NOT IGNORE THE NEED TO PRUNE JUDICIOUSLY

I noticed the English Yews in front of some low windows were covering those windows, so off I went to get the loppers. Once I started, I could not stop. The more I pruned, the worse they looked. I got them down to ugly stumps, and it was then I realized I had to hire a landscaper to pull the shrubs out and plant new ones. Yes, a costly pruning lesson.

CHAPTER ELEVEN
SOME PERENNIAL FAVORITES

SOME OF MY FAVORITE PERENNIALS:

Flowers:

- Skating Party - a super white flowering bearded iris
- Aster Frikartii - blue flowers that grow one-to-two feet and is long blooming. Pinch back in the spring and again one month later which develops more flowers
- Casa Blanca Lily - white flowers
- David White Phlox - resists mildew
- Kaemferi Iris - late blooming
- Aenome - September charm
- Gaura
- Crocosmia Lucifer
- Achillea Anthea Yarrow - a lighter yellow than moonshine

Shrub:

Evergreen
- Pinus Strobus variety
- Blue Shag – low-growing place in full sun
- Acantha Panax variegates
- False Aralia yellow and green foliage - great shade plant

Tree:
- White birch - white spire does not get borers - white trunk but no exfoliating

CHAPTER TWELVE

EVERGREENS AND SOME ANNUALS

WONDERS OF THE GARDEN

Some Evergreens are deer resistant which is essential with the thriving deer population throughout the country. Here is a list of some of the most deer resistant:

- Korean Boxwood – Fertilize in the fall with Holly-tone or Plant-tone to achieve a good green color
- English Boxwood – Fertilize in the fall with Holly-tone or Plant-tone to achieve a good green color
- Cherry Laurel
- Otto lykens
- Spruce
- Hemlock
- Grasses
- Juniper
- Fir
- Chamacyparis (conifer in the Cypress genus)
- Cehpholotaxus (also a conifer that resembles yews)

OTHER BLOOMS THAT WILL MAKE YOU SIT UP AND TAKE NOTICE

Gartenmeister Annual Fuschia – an upright salmon-colored has showy colorful flowers and grows well in shaded areas and attracts hummingbirds.

Rozanne – a perennial plant, this hybrid Geranium works well when used in the front of the border. It blooms all season. It seems to disappear in colder months, but comes back for many years and the blue variety is lovely.

Richmondii Begonia – an annual that makes a super hanging plant that can grow and flourish in moderate to deep shade.

SOME TREES THAT CAN POSE A PROBLEM OR BE PEST PRONE

- Mountain Ash
- Honey Locust
- Female Genko
- Norway Maple
- Black Walnut (this has toxic roots)

***

My husband Bob and I retired to Brewster, Cape Cod and bought a 200-year-old captain's house with an out building and no gardens.

I renovated the out building and opened a fabulous shop selling antiques and unusual plant containers and garden accents. The shop was unique on the Cape.

Then I started to build gardens on the three-quarter acre barren lot. First, I planted large perennial gardens followed by a rose garden then followed by a shade garden. I finished off with a sunken garden with a water feature and my very own Secret Garden. I placed items from the shop around all the gardens.

Customers came to not only buy from the antique shop but to see how the items worked in the gardens. After the customers walked the gardens, they often asked me to design gardens for their properties which I thoroughly enjoyed.

CHAPTER THIRTEEN

SHADE GARDENING

And

SOIL PREPARATION

A shade garden is often cultivated below large trees which makes it difficult to grow plants. To rectify this problem, build a soil mound about 13 inches high. This small amount will not damage tree roots and it will allow the planting of a shade garden.

Plant four to six-inch plants in individual holes. This allows the roots of the young plants to find their way into the surrounding soil. Smaller plants adapt to the shade better than larger ones.

Prolific Plants and Shrubs for Shade Gardens:

Perennials:

- Hostas
- Painted Fern (Lovely)
- Solomon Seal
- Tradescantia (White variety is especially nice but cut it down after flowering as it can be invasive.)
- Foxglove (biennial)
- Bleeding Heart (When the leaves yellow, cut it back)
- Geranium Maculate (Light shade)
- Jacobs Ladder
- Thalictrum
- Ligularia
- Liriope
- Astilbe
- Hellebores

- Epimediums

Annual Plants:

- Impatiens
- Begonias
- Streptocarpus
- Coleus

Shrubs for Shade:

- Kerria (Deciduous and blooms after Forsythia)
- Manhattan Euymous (Evergreen)
- Viburnum Trilobum
- Cranberry High Bush (Deciduous)
- Cryptomeria (Evergreen)
- Native Rhododendrum (Evergreen)
- Pieris Japonica (Evergreen
- Blue Princess Holly (Must have the male Blue Prince to Berry)
- Buxus Microphylla (Evergreen)
- Grape Mahonia (Evergreen)
- Cherry Laurel Otto Lykens Dwarf or (Low Growing Variety)
- Cherry Laurel Laurocerasus Schipkoensis (Tall Variety)

CHAPTER FOURTEEN

CONTAINER GARDENS

OR

BIG BLOOMS IN SMALL SPACES

Container gardening creates a full garden in a small space. Containers need the right soil, flowers and care if they are to achieve their optimum beauty. There are many types of containers and the ones listed below can withstand all types of weather and temperatures.

THERE ARE MANY TYPES OF CONTAINERS

STONE

CAST IRON

CAST ALUMINUM

ITALIAN CLAY

FIBRE GLASS

FAUX

CERAMICS FROM VIETNAM

CONTAINER TIPS:

- Wet a new clay pot before planting. This helps the clay retain moisture which in turn helps prevent the soil from drying once you plant flowers.
- Spray stone pots with Thompson's water sealer before use.
- If you live in a cold climate, other ceramics and clay containers must be put away in cold storage for the winter or emptied of soil and turned over

in place.

- Plan where you want to use containers and what type of containers you like before you purchase flowers.

- Make sure that you keep up with the watering of your containers. Buy a water metering device which can be found at garden centers and many stores. It can help you determine when your plants need water.

- Do not water in the evening after the sun has gone down as there is no immediate need for water at this time. It could lead to the growth of fungi or bacteria especially in the spring or fall.

- Select plants that require similar watering practices.

- Try not to combine fast growing plants with slow growing plants in the same containers.

- Plant in the spring to let the feeder roots get established because this is when they absorb the nutrients and water.

- Water the container usually twice a week and then fertilize with blossom booster such as Miracle-Gro® once a week. If the container contains flowering plants, add the blossom booster into a two-gallon watering can.

- Make sure your container has holes for drainage. Cover the hole or holes with fine screening or landscape cloth.

COMMON PLACES TO USE CONTAINERS:

Containers add beauty to a stone wall when lined up atop of the wall. They add dimension to terrace or patio, and they pave the way to the entrance of a garden. They can even be used in a perennial garden to add dimension and decoration.

When using several containers in a given area, I suggest you use only two types of containers together so your containers live in harmony with the gardens around them or on the terrace or patio or walkway. I find that solid-colored containers work best with all flowers. If your containers are near a perennial garden, use the same color flowers in the container that you have in the perennial garden so that the container flowers do not conflict with the garden blooms.

CHOOSING A CONTAINER:

When choosing your container, examine the space where it will be placed. You want that container to make a big impact and bigger containers are fine as long as the area can handle that size planter.

NOTE: The bigger the container the less time it will take to dry out.

Try to use large and medium-sized planters as much as possible because using many small planters can look haphazard and confuse the eye and take away from the beauty of your flowers.

TYPES OF SOIL FOR CONTAINERS

Soilless Soil

Soilless growing mediums are cleaner and less likely to be bothered by pests which is why many container gardeners prefer this type of "soil." In truth, there is no soil in these mixtures. There are organic and inorganic materials which save many plants in containers from dirt or soil-prone diseases

POTTING SOIL WITH FERTILIZER

For containers, I prefer to use potting soil and add my recipe of fertilizers. My favorite concoction is to add Osmocote, Plant-tone, Super Phosphate and Soil Moist.

To a 20-pound bag of potting soil, I add one cup of each of the ingredients above and three tablespoons of soil moist because it does what it says and keeps the soil moist.

If you have existing containers and wish to add Soil Moist to them, make several holes into the soil with the end of a pencil and add the proper amount of the mixture.

10-INCH HANGING BASKET	2 TEASPOONS
1 GALLON	2 TEASPOONS
3 GALLON	3 TEASPOONS
5 GALLON	2 TABLESPOONS
10 GALLON	4 TABLESPOONS

After planting in any of these soilless mixtures, add Blossom Booster once a week.

Container plants are usually planted with annual flowers. These types of blooms need weekly fertilization as the containers are constantly being watered which drains the nutrients from the plants.

Super Thrive is not a fertilizer but it does allow the roots to grow fuller rather than wrapping them around the inside of the container. To me this is like a steroid for plants.

If you are fertilizing correctly and your plants are not responding, a tablespoon of lime will help the soil release the fertilizer.

Bush and standard Hibiscus are two of the most common plants used in containers because they continually bloom. These plants need a consistent fertilization program, and I have detailed it below:

Sprinkle one tablespoon of granular Super Phosphate to the soil once a month. Also add soluble Blossom Booster weekly as well as Ironite another week in the month. They are high-maintenance plants but their beauty proves they are worth the trouble.

***

Back to the Cape Cod Shop

One day my husband Bob was manning the shop. When I returned, he told me that he had sold two iron plant stands, and he gave me a check for the sale. When I saw the amount, I noticed it was for half the amount of what the two stands would cost. Yes, there was only one tag, but he assumed the tag covered both stands. If I mentioned his error to him, her would never have entered the shop again.

***

I received a request to develop a roof top garden at a

Philadelphia hospital. Of course, I was up for the challenge, but it was a bigger challenge than I had anticipated. The area was a barren black top. I had to bring in all the plants, stone, mulch, containers and soil. An irrigation set up also had to be brought to the area through a window. The window could only handle a 20-inch container. My team and I were continually in and out of that one window. It was physically and emotionally exhausting. When it was completed, I received another request for the same type of garden. I knew better now and asked the potential client what was the access to the area. They replied that it was the same situation as the garden we just completed. I said thank you but no thank you.
That was a one and done deal.

***

Lessons with Fertilizer

When fertilizing, too much is as bad as too little.

I was asked to design and plant a perennial garden. This was my first design. I prepared the soil and added the fertilizer. I planted the plants and thought, "Why not add some more fertilizer?"

The plants grew and looked quite lush, but the flowers were sparse. This told me that I had given the garden too much nitrogen fertilizer which grows lush green foliage but few flowers. Another lesson learned.

CHAPTER FIFTEEN
HOUSE PLANT TIPS

Live plants bring the rather sterile indoor environment to life. They fill that open space in your room that looks as if it is begging for something warm and alive. You know you want plants, but what plants should you select and where do you want them in the house?

Certain plants take more light than others to survive in an indoor situation. For example, a Ficus tree or Fig tree, takes moderate to high light. If a Ficus tree has been grown in an outside environment—say in Florida—and it is accustomed to all that sun, it will flourish and grow quickly in that warm sun. Unfortunately, when that same Ficus arrives at a nursery in a less tropical environment, it usually sheds a lot of leaves.

How do I keep my indoor plants healthy? Here are some tips on a keeping your indoor plants healthy and happy.

- To water or not water is the big question in the life of indoor plants. This is a difficult question, and that is why a plant water meter is a great help. It determines the dryness or wetness of the soil. It is a guide, but common sense is necessary. And a tip to protect your floors or carpet: When placing a plant in a decorative container, put a deep saucer under the plant to contain the runoff of water.

- A plant breathes through its leaves. It takes the carbon dioxide from the atmosphere and gives off oxygen. This is why you need to wash the plant leaves to keep their Stomata (the opening in the

leaves) clear. A good leaf spray to clean plants is
Pokon.

- If the plants have yellow leaves, it may mean you
  are overwatering. If they are dropping green leaves,
  you need to water.

- Keeping many plants together increases the
  humidity in the area which is beneficial to plants.
  If placing two plants together, choose the same
  variety. If placing three plants together, use two of
  the same variety and one other variety.

- Plants prefer air movement and cool, not hot air.
  With cool air, the plants are not as susceptible to
  disease and insects.

- To fertilize or not to fertilize? Indoor plants need
  to be fertilized once a year with a fertilizer high in
  nitrogen.

- Plants in an indoor environment need to be checked
  once a week for watering. Only water if necessary,
  they like a substantial or thorough drink. When
  you water, take note if water comes out quickly. If
  water does exit quickly, it is an indication that the
  plant went too dry. During watering, if the plant
  does not drain and water puddles on top of the soil,
  it probably did not need a drink.

- Be careful when choosing your indoor plants. Keep in mind that different plants have differing light requirements. Usually most indoor plants are chosen for a low-light environment, such as Pathos, Dracena Janet Craig, Dracena Warnecki, Neanthe Bella and Kentia Palm. For an area with a lot of natural light, a Ficus tree, Chinese Evergreen or Bamboo palm will do nicely.

CHAPTER SIXTEEN

CARE OF THE ROSE

Romantic and beautiful

Few flowers are held in such high esteem as the rose. The health of rose bushes depend upon the soil in which they are planted. Here are some tips on growing healthy roses:

- The soil should consist of one-third weed-free loam, one-third sand, one-third humus (organic matter) and dehydrated cow manure
- When planting a rose bush, mix some of the fertilizers into the soil of the planting hole as well as water and a one-third cup each of Super Phosphate and Plant-One
- Keep in mind that proper drainage and sufficient organic matter ensures the soil has the ability to retain moisture and a steady supply of nutrients to help the growth of the rose. Also, having some clay in the soil will help water retention.
- Roses need at least one inch of water per week. When rose bushes become dry, their growth slows and they produce fewer blossoms.
- Pruning is a necessity in order to keep roses healthy. In general, prune away dead wood and open the middle of the bush to allow light and air throughout. You can prune safely in early spring or fall.

THE CARE FOR ROSES

The **Hybrid Tea Rose,** which is perhaps the most popular, is tall and stately with large blossoms and long stems. In the spring or fall, prune the canes to above 15 inches leaving three to five canes producing a vase-type effect.

In the spring, remove debris from the beds and also from the soil mounds. Use a fungicide spray on the cuts to protect against air-borne diseases. Remove spent blooms cutting them to just above a cluster of the five leaves.

Another variety of rose is the **Floribunder**. You can prune this rose the same as the Hybrid Tea, but leave about eight or nine healthy canes.

Knock Out Roses can be pruned in the spring or fall. Cut out any dead wood. How much you prune depends upon how and where it is grown. If it is viewed from a distance, let it grown full and tall. If it is being grown as a hedge, you decide how tall and full you want it to be. This rose can be grown in full or moderate sun. It will also bloom all summer and into the fall with little care if you keep up with the deadheading.

Miniature Roses are quite useful in limited spaces and can grow to up to three feet. Prune these dainty blossoms to the desired height being mindful of the area in which they are grown

Landscape Roses are grown as small bushes and require little care. They can be pruned in the fall to the ground or to half their size. With casual deadheading they bloom all summer and into the fall.

Rosa Rugosa – After this bush flowers, thin and remove older canes. The plants should be pruned to the ground in the spring or fall.

Tree Roses are usually grown in containers and require the same care as all other roses. They can be stored for the winter in a basement near a window or even in a garage with artificial light. Water sparingly.

ROSE SOIL HEALTH

The pH of the soil is vital to the growth of the roots of roses. Roses are unable to take up the nutrients from any soil that is too acid or too alkaline. Roses prefer a pH between 5.5 and 7.0 (neutral). A pH that is reasonably acidic produces beautiful blossoms. Soil acidity can change rapidly so be sure to check the pH in the spring. Add lime to raise the pH and add Sulphur or sphagnum peat moss to lower the ph.

Again, remember that garden centers have devices that test the pH of soil or if you prefer, you can send a sample to your state extension service which will test the pH of your soil.

Keep in mind that if you have well water, your soil might be more alkaline.

SUNLIGHT

Most roses prefer four to six hours of direct sunlight daily. A location that receives morning sun helps to deter mildew.

ROSE BEDS

When planting roses, give them a bed of their own as it allows better control of the proper fertilization and watering program.

FERTILIZING ROSES

At the first sign of leaves on the rose bush, apply one-half to three-quarters of a cup of granular rose food such as Bayer Advanced Rose and Flower Care which feeds and protects against insects. Apply it around the drip line or the area defined by the outermost circumference of the plant canopy where water drips from and onto the ground, and scratch it in being careful not to disturb the roots. Then water.

In May, add a second application in the same way as the first was applied. In June, you can do a third application and in July, a fourth. In August, you will make your final application.

The fall requires some rose care as well. In October apply one-half to three-quarters of a cup of granular Super Phosphate around the drip lines. This is for root growth in the late season and for the following spring.

After the first hard frost of the fall, mound the soil around the base of your Hybrid Tea Roses. Do no gather soil from the base of the rose as you may damage the roots. A good practice would be to store some soil in your garden shed to keep it from freezing so you can mound it around the roses.

When adding a rose to an established soil, add and mix into the soil one-third cup of Super Phosphate.

WATERING ROSES

A well-watered rose has a better chance to survive a wind storm or an autumn drought. Until the soil freezes, keep watering your roses! The more green, healthy leaves you have on your roses, the more blossoms you will have.

PREVENTING BLACK SPOT AND MILDEW

As soon as the roses start to leaf out in the spring, start your spray schedule to deter black spot, mildew and other diseases:

Mix one tablespoon of fungicide and one tablespoon of white vinegar in a gallon of water. Spray the undersides as well as the tops of the leaves. Try and do this when you are not expecting rain for at least 24 hours.

This spray program should be repeated weekly through the growing season. This is especially necessary for **Hybrid Tea Roses** as well as **Floribunda**

The spray is unnecessary for Knock Out Roses and Landscape Roses unless a problem arises.

PEST ATTACKS

Aphids seem to attack new growth on most roses but you can blast them off the buds with a strong spray of the hose. If they are persistent, use a Safer's soap solution or a dormant oil, which are sprays refined from petroleum oil or cottonseed oil that have an emulsifier added to allow the oil to mix with water.

Another treatment is to dissolve one and a half-crushed aspirin tablets into a gallon of water. Aspirin is salicylic acid, a substance that plants make naturally to defend against bacteria, fungi and viruses. Spray the solution on the plants and water the roots with it as well. Repeat once a month only so you do not burn the plant.

Applying the aspiring solution speeds up the process of a systemic acquired resistance response.

Lastly, keep roses always free of debris. Any leaves with black spot fungus spores left lying on the ground will re-infect the bush.

CHAPTER SEVENTEEN
CARE OF THE LILY

True lilies are perennial plants growing from bulbs which produce tall leafy stems resulting in a terminal flower or flowers. Two of the most beautiful lilies are **Casablanca** and **Star Gazer.**

There are other plants that are called lilies but do not really belong to the true lily genus such as the Daylily, Calla Lily and the Plantain Lily.

The growing season for the many varieties of lilies is from May to late September, and the flowers can last from eight to ten weeks.

Lilies are long-lived, hardy plants and great care should be taken in planting them. These perennials may also be purchased in pots in the growing season and will bloom again next season allowing you to see their color and size of flower. If ordered bare-rooted, lilies should have at least some of their roots intact.

LILY SOIL HEALTH, FERTILIZING AND PLANTING

Lilies require a slightly acidic soil with plenty of humus. The soil should drain well so that the roots will not rot and fail in too moist soil. If you have heavy wet soil, mix a handful of coarse sand into the bottom of the hole before planting and on top of the bulb to help with the drainage. You can also add dehydrated cow manure mixed in with the existing soil.

With proper care, lilies rarely need to be transplanted unless they become crowded by other plants.

If you have ordered or purchased Lily bulbs from a nursery, keep them in a cool area and slightly damp—but not wet. If they have arrived in a plastic bag, remove them immediately. Daffodils and tulips can be kept out of the soil longer than Lilies. It is best to plant the Lilies as soon as they arrive.

Plant the bulbs in a group of three to five and plant them six to twelve inches apart at a depth of six to seven inches.

Lilies like the morning sun and some shade from the midday sun. This amount of light allows the flowers to bloom longer. If you would like to cut a species bloom, cut one-third of the stem as this gives the bulb the opportunity will bloom again next season.

Fertilize the Lilies in the spring with a top dressing of Plant-tone and spread it away from the base of the Lily. In December or January, add a light dressing of Super Phosphate.

After your Lily has bloomed, remove old flowers as they fade. This prevents the plant from going to seed which reduces the flower production for the following season.

LILY PESTS AND PROBLEMS

Wet foliage and a hot sun produce spotting on the leaves.

The Lily Leaf Beetle can be a large problem. It does not live in all areas, but be aware. This beetle has a black head and an orange to red body. Symptoms of the beetle include holes in the leaves which will kill next year's flowers.

The insecticide Neem is most effective against newly-hatched Lily Leaf Beetle larvae. You can also knock down the adult beetles and trap them into a container holding one inch of soapy water. To protect your Lilies, it is best to get the beetles before they reach the adult stage.

If you see the Lily Leaf Beetle species emerging in the spring, spray with Bayer Advanced Rose and Flower pray and also apply it to the soil around the lily.

CHAPTER EIGHTEEN
THE CARE OF THE DAYLILY

When planting a Daylily, work together in the planting hole, soil and some granular Super Phosphate fertilizer. Do not plant too deeply as this inhibits growth and flowering.

If the plant looks good and blooms well, do not give it more fertilizer. On the other hand, if it is not producing blooms and looks tired, give it a small amount of dehydrated cow manure or fish emulsion during the blooming season.

Hold back on a Nitrogen fertilizer as too much stimulates green growth and the plants grow too fast to bloom well.

Spread Plant-tone around established plants in the spring.

Daylily plants grow best in the sun to light shade. They need plenty of water which helps to produce new flowers each day during the growing season.

Deadheading is necessary to prevent seed pods from forming and the plants look better.

***

I tried to keep my Cape Cod Shop open 11-5 every day. Some days I would be called away and then I had to close.

The fact that the shop was not always open did not make for happy customers.
Therefore, I decided to keep the shop open even when there was no one in the shop.

A note was placed in a prominently placed container. Stating, "If you have to have it now, leave cash or check and 6% sales tax".

To my delight upon returning, I found cash or checks and sometimes a note saying they were delighted to find the shop always open.

Honesty and a love of plants go a long way!

CHAPTER NINETEEN
CARE OF THE IRIS

The Iris are perennial herbs with sword-like leaves and roots that are rhizomatous or fibrous.

There are many varieties and the bloom time varies with each variety. In the early spring, the Bulbous Iris is first to bloom followed by the Siberian Iris which has strong fibrous roots. The Glorious Bearded Iris grown from a rhizome is next to show off its beauty and finally the Japanese Iris or the Kaempferia, which also has strong fibrous roots, blooms a bit later in the spring.

IRIS SOIL HEALTH, FERTILIZING AND PLANTING

Good plant practice is vital especially for the Bearded Iris as it may get borers. Spray the plant with an insecticide when the leaves are six to eight inches high. Do this in the first and third week of May.

Borers are caused by the pink larva of a cutworm moth. The larva lay eggs on top of the leaf (This looks like a line down the leaf). The eggs bore into the rhizome causing it to become soft and mushy.

If leaves are falling over and displaying a bit of yellow, check the rhizome for basil rot. If you see evidence of borers, dig the infected plant after it blooms and cut out the mushy areas of the rhizome until you get a nice firm rhizome

To plant a single rhizome, dig a deep hole and make a mound of soil even in the planting hole. Place the rhizome on top of the mound and then spread its roots down around the mound. Fill the hole with soil and firm it so there are no air pockets. You should be able to see the rhizome and then cover it with one quarter inch of soil.

Bearded Iris can be dug up after July and divided any time after they bloom. When dividing the plants, use a blunt knife and plunge the blade down one or two inches. Then push the blade up and down to release the rhizome. A low nitrogen fertilizer may be applied to the Bearded Iris twice. First in the early spring as growth starts and then in the late summer to stimulate fall growth. A water-soluble Blossom Booster fertilizer should be applied in early June. A small amount of granular Super Phosphate should be applied in January or February. This should be purchased in the summer as garden centers usually don't carry it in the winter months. All fertilizers are put on as a side dressing not directly on the rhizome. Be careful to not put too much fertilizer as that can result in soft growth which may leave the plant vulnerable to disease.

If mulch is used, do not put directly on the center of the plant, surround it instead and spread it around.

In the early spring, plant Bulbous Iris three to four inches deep.

The Siberian Iris has a strong fibrous root system so when planting, dig a large hold and reinforce it with dehydrated cow manure which is mixed into the planting hole. It is important to remove the seed pods of the Siberian Iris as the larvae of several insects mature in these pods. This plant is a heavy feeder and needs plenty of water while it is producing its flowers. It also likes a pH of 5.5 to 6.5.

A well-established plant will form a good-sized clump and should be divided in three to four years.

WHERE ARE THE BLOOMS?

After doing all the right cultural practices, some gardeners notice their Bearded Iris do not bloom. Why?

- They might have become overcrowded and need to be divided and replanted in the fall.
- Is the rhizome almost on the top of the soil?
- If you have an abundance of green leaves and no flowers, you may be using too much nitrogen fertilizer. Scatter some granular Super Phosphate around the area being very careful not to put it directly on the rhizome.

I cannot say enough about the product Milorganite as a super deer deterrent. It works

CHAPTER TWENTY
THE CARE OF THE CYMBIDIUM ORCHID

Cymbidiums make such a striking statement when in bloom. Start with a medium-sized plant and place it in either a solid black, brass or silver container. Then set it on the entry table or other prominent spot in your home and enjoy its beauty.

Cymbidiums have a once a year bloom period that lasts between eight and ten weeks. When your orchid is no longer in bloom, let the plant become very dry before watering. Water only when the growing medium is dry. Place it in the sun if possible or at least where there is a good, strong light.

CARE OF YOUR CYMBIDIUM

In the spring, place the orchid outside in a semi-shaded area and fertilize it weekly with a high-nitrogen fertilizer. The nitrogen level is the first number on the fertilizer container. Follow the directions on how much fertilizer to add to a gallon of water and then proceed to water your orchid weekly.

From August until the temperature drops to about 40 degrees, substitute the high-nitrogen fertilizer with a Blossom Booster which has the numbers 0-30-10. Follow the directions on the Blossom Booster to see how much fertilizer should be added to a gallon of water.

Plants like to be watered and then they like to dry out and then need to be watered again. The growing medium of the orchid should not be soggy, but it should not be totally dry either. In other words, an evenly moist medium is preferred.

During the cooler periods, water in the morning so it can dry out before the lower night temperatures hit.

If the orchid is getting too much or too little light, the color of the leaves will tip you off right away. The leaves should be bright green.

CHAPTER TWENTY-ONE

GLADIOLA, SPRING BULBS and HYDRANGEA

Beautiful Blooms for Bouquets

Plant Gladiola corms in the spring. Make sure to always purchase a firm, good-sized corm. Gladiolas prefer a soil mixture containing peat moss and sand.

The planting depth of the corm should be two times the size of the corm. Be sure to plant these flowers in full sun. Water two to three times per week sparingly to avoid rotting the corm. Gladiolas should bloom in about six weeks. For continual bloom, plant more corms every six weeks. Gladiolas are lovely cut flowers.

CARING AND FERTILIZING FOR GLADIOLA SPRING BULBS

After the spring bulbs flower, the foliage should remain so that they can collect carbohydrates and solar rays for the photosynthetic process.

Bulbs that were planted in the fall should be fertilized in the spring to encourage new growth and spring bulbs.

Add dehydrated cow manure and fish emulsion plus a small amount of 5-10-5 fertilizer and water into the soil.

HIBISCUS CULTURE

When well cared for, Hibiscus grow quite well in containers. To keep them in continual bloom, it is necessary to follow a weekly fertilizing schedule.

Plant the Hibiscus in a good soil mixture of one-part garden soil, one-part dehydrated cow manure and one-part sand or perlite lightener.

A 12-inch container is a good size for the Hibiscus. When planting in a container, mix into the soil one tablespoon of Osmocote, one tablespoon of Plant-tone and a half teaspoon of soil moist. After planting the Hibiscus, water well and place in full sun.

MONTHLY FERTILIZING SCHEDULE

Week One: Spread one tablespoon of granular Super Phosphate on the soil and water.

Week Two: Fertilize with a nitrogen fertilizer such as Ironite. Follow the directions as to the amount of fertilizer to use. Do not fertilize a dry plant. Make sure the soil of the plant is damp before fertilizing

Week Three: Use a soluble Blossom Booster with a 15-30-15 ratio.

Week Four: Use clear water

Always remove spent blossoms. Prune as you see fit to keep the plant in the size and shape you desire.

Hibiscus containers can be held over the winter in a heated

or unheated garage near a window or artificial light. Water occasionally as you want to keep the plant alive for the spring.

HYDRANGEA CULTURE

The Hydrangea shrub is one of the most widely used and most beautiful. The Hydrangea is deciduous which means it loses its leaves in cold climates; therefore, it is not the best choice for foundation planting.

These plants can be grown in full sun or light shade. If grown in full sun, they will need to be watched more carefully as to their watering needs. Their favorite growing space is in light shade or morning sun.

Grow these plants in moist, well-drained soil. The soil should consist of garden soil, peat moss, dehydrated cow manure and a bit of coarse sand.

As soon as the plant shows new growth in the spring, scatter a cupful of 5-10-5 Plant-tone and dehydrated cow manure at the base of the plant and add water.

In July, fertilize with a liquid feed of Blossom Booster with a 15-30-15 ratio such as Miracle-Gro) Add one scoop to a gallon of water. Do not fertilize after September 1st.

In January, spread Super Phosphate at the base of the plant. If there is snow on the ground, spread it on top of the snow.

To produce pink flowers, the pH should be 6.0 to 6.5. To achieve this color display, spread ground limestone on the soil around the base of the plant—a cupful should do the trick. Do this as soon as the plant starts to grow and then add water immediately.

To achieve blue flowers, the pH should be between 5.0 and 5.5. For this color display, scatter one cup of Aluminum Sulphate around the base of the plant as soon as the plant starts to grow. Repeat this practice two times at two-week intervals and water.

Buy Hydrangeas in the spring when they are in bloom so you can verify their color.

When you prune in the spring, remove the storm-damaged branches and dead wood. **Do not cut the plant to the ground. If you cut to the ground, the plant will not bloom that season. Prune the stems that have carried flowers. When removing the bloom, prune above the second node. The first node on the stem is blind. Do not prune new shoots.**

When cutting flowers for a floral display, add a bit of mild detergent and a teaspoon of sugar to hot water. This will help the blooms last longer.

Prune Oak-leaved Hydrangeas after they bloom. Prune the

dead flowers, but do not severely prune. In the spring, fertilize with Blossom Booster add one scoop to two gallons of water.

CHAPTER TWENTY-TWO
GROWING THAT TOMATO

Tomatoes are one of the most popular vegetables to grow. Is there anything better to a gardener than plucking that first ripe tomato off the vine? A ripe tomato is not only beautiful to look at, but it contains fiber, iron, magnesium, a variety of vitamins and the antioxidant lycopene, and it tastes great.

GROWING TOMATOES

Tomatoes don't need much room to grow. You can grow them in containers or in a small patch of garden.

Prepare the soil by adding compost (organic matter) or mushroom soil if you can obtain this. Work the compost material into the existing soil along with tomato fertilizer.

If you are planting tomatoes in your garden, begin by digging a hole after the last frost. Add the soil mixture and a support for the vine. Mulch the area and give the plants about two gallons of water per week.

If you are planting your tomatoes in a container, purchase a good-sized on that allows your plant plenty of room to grow. You can use a soilless mixture, but keep in mind that this mixture dries out quickly, so it requires more maintenance. So, if time is a factor, garden soil is the best choice for growing tomatoes.

Buy young plants that are about eight inches tall. Do not buy plants with yellow leaves or thin, scraggly stems.

Tomatoes need plenty of sunshine to thrive. Fertilize the

plants with a tomato fertilizer every two weeks.

If you see tiny shoots in the leaf axles, pinch them out as this allows better growth for the fruit. When the top of the plant has grown to four flower branches, pinch it off. This allows your tomatoes to ripen fruit rather than growing taller

A steady supply of water is necessary to keep tomatoes healthy. Do not let these plants go dry.

If you see holes in the tomatoes, you might have a caterpillar feeding on the fruit. These insects are big and green and cling to the stem, so they can be difficult to see. When you find them, pick them off, cut them in half or drown them. Yes, it sounds pretty awful, but it is necessary to keep your plants safe.

ASPIRIN SOLUTION

Aspirin is a Salicylic Acid substance that plants make to trigger a natural defense against bacteria, fungi and viruses. Applying an aspirin solution speeds up the resistance response.

To make a solution: Dissolve one-and-a-half crushed, regular aspirin into a gallon of water. Spray it on the plants and then water the roots of the plant with the remaining solution. Use this solution once a month. Using it too often can burn the plants.

CHAPTER TWENTY-THREE

A STORY FOR THE YOUNG GARDENERS

Early one morning, Mr. Crunch went out to his large garden to pick some vegetables. He wanted fresh lettuce and some carrots.

"Oh my!" Mr. Crunch exclaimed. "A lot of the lettuce has already been picked. And where are the carrots?"

What could have happened to Mr. Crunch's garden?

Mr. Crunch knew that bunnies like to eat lettuce and carrots but he had not seen any bunnies in his garden and that was strange since he went to the garden each day. What should he do?

He had to find out who or what was eating his lettuce and carrots. So later that day, quiet as a mouse, Mr. Crunch walked around to the back of the garden. He stayed very quiet. There he saw three fat bunnies. They were there with their baskets hopping along and filling their baskets.

"What are you doing?" shouted Mr. Crunch.

Surprised, the bunnies jumped up and Mr. Crunch saw their baskets were filled.

The fattest of the three bunnies bowed to Mr. Crunch and said, "Pardon us, Sir. I am Whippy and these are my two friends Dippy and Flippy."

"I am Mr. Crunch and this is my garden, and I don't like anyone picking the vegetables without asking me first."

Flippy looked at his two friends and then to Mr. Crunch.

"I'm afraid we have a problem Mr. Crunch."

"What might that be," the gardener asked.

"Let's all go over to our cottage that is just behind the garden and talk about it," said the bunny.

To get to the cottage was no big deal for the bunnies, but Mr. Crunch had to crawl on his hands and knees. When he finally squirmed his way into the cottage, he saw the three bunnies sitting on a stone bench waiting for him. They offered him a very small stool to sit upon, but Mr. Crunch could not get comfortable as his knees were hitting his chin. He stopped fidgeting and said,

"You called this chat, so what is the problem you were talking about?"

The three bunnies asked him to look around the cottage. Their sitting area was quite small and it had a stone floor. They had nowhere to grow vegetables.

"We like your garden," Whippy said. "We like to gather our food from your garden and scurry about and play hide-and-seek. We like the flowers that grow near your garden too."

As Mr. Crunch observed the three bunnies and their filled baskets, he said "I guess we all need a plan we can live with. Why don't we meet here tomorrow at tea time? I will bring the fixings for our tea—lettuce for you and cookies for me. I think we can be great friends."

That night Mr. Crunch did not sleep very well. He was trying to think of a solution for the garden. The next day at tea, the bunnies looked worried. Would they be able to pick from the garden? What would they do for food?

Mr. Crunch decided to plant a garden just for the bunnies near their cottage. He would build a fence around the garden so his garden would be protected and the bunnies would be safe in their own space. He promised to plant lettuce and carrots and other vegetables the bunnies liked. The bunnies jumped with excitement and gratitude.

The very next day, Mr. Crunch began the bunnies' new garden. He planted the seeds in a sunny area of his yard near their cottage and he set up a watering system because he knew that for the vegetables to grow, they needed dirt, sunlight and water.

He taught Dippy, Flippy and Whippy how to tend to their garden and they grew lots of food to fill their baskets. Mr. Crunch and the bunnies shared the land and with two gardens, there was enough food for all.

AUTHOR BIO:

After graduating from college, Pat went to work in the personnel division of the Jordan Marsh Co. in Boston, Massachusetts.

She married and she and her husband had three children who are all grown along with two grandchildren. Originally, she was a stay-at-home mom who became involved in many community activities including the Girl Scouts where she served as troop leader.

When her children entered high school, she started a company which focused on interior and exterior plant design and maintenance. She designed gardens and lectured about gardening on Cape Cod and on the Mainline outside Philadelphia where she lived in the town of Wayne for more than 27 years. She also designed and lectured in Memphis, Tennessee and Bloomfield Hills, Michigan. Pat attended the Barnes Horticultural Institute in Philadelphia for 3 years.

Eventually, she retired to Cape Cod, Massachusetts and opened a store selling antique and unusual plant containers and garden accents as well as designing and installing perennial gardens.

She still spends part of the winter on an island off the coast of Belize, Central America designing gardens and teaching proper maintenance of gardens.

Made in the USA
Lexington, KY
25 November 2019

57645994R00061